DATE DUE

I Can Draw
COUNTRY
Animals

Please visit our web site at: **www.garethstevens.com**
For a free color catalog describing Gareth Stevens' list of high-quality books and multimedia programs, call 1-800-542-2595 (USA) or 1-800-461-9120 (Canada). Gareth Stevens Publishing's Fax: (414) 332-3567.

Library of Congress Cataloging-in-Publication Data

Leroux-Hugon, Hélène.
    [Animaux de la campagne. English]
    I can draw country animals / by Hélène Leroux-Hugon.
        p. cm. — (I can draw animals!)
    Includes bibliographical references and index.
    ISBN 0-8368-2838-0 (lib. bdg.)
    1. Animals in art—Juvenile literature. 2. Drawing—Technique—Juvenile
literature. [1. Animals in art. 2. Drawing—Technique.] I. Title.
NC780.L3913   2001
743.6'9—dc21   00-053147

This edition first published in 2001 by
Gareth Stevens Publishing
A World Almanac Education Group Company
330 West Olive Street, Suite 100
Milwaukee, Wisconsin 53212 USA

This U.S. edition © 2001 by Gareth Stevens, Inc. Original edition first published by Larousse-Bordas, Paris, France, under the title *Les animaux de la Campagne*, © Dessain et Tolra/HER 2000. Additional end matter © 2001 by Gareth Stevens, Inc.

Illustrations: Hélène Leroux-Hugon
Photography: Cactus Studio
Translation: Valerie J. Weber
English text: Valerie J. Weber
Gareth Stevens editor: Katherine Meitner
Cover design: Katherine Kroll

Printed in the United States of America

1 2 3 4 5 6 7 8 9 05 04 03 02 01

I Can Draw
COUNTRY
Animals

Hélène Leroux-Hugon

Gareth Stevens Publishing
A WORLD ALMANAC EDUCATION GROUP COMPANY

Table of Contents

I Can Draw

Observing

Look at the animals around you, without pencil or paper. This will help you see animals in a different way. Try to find some simple shapes in these animals — for example, a circle for a head or an oval for a body.

Practicing

Without using a stencil or a compass, draw circles, ovals, and curves by hand. This is called freestyle drawing. Notice that your circles may not be perfectly round and that an oval can be wide or narrow, short or long.

Drawing by Steps

Now choose your model in the book. A cat might be good. There are many cats in the city and in the countryside, where you can easily watch them.

1 The cat is made up of an oval for the body and another oval for the head (see page 8). Step by step, draw the form, making a light mark with your pencil. At first, of course, your drawing will be simple. This stage is called a sketch; it helps you see the size of the head compared to the size of the body and where each body part should go.

2   Add the front and back legs. Don't press on your pencil too hard because you're going to make several marks before deciding which one is the best. You will have to erase the marks shown as dotted lines on the model.

3   Draw the ears, the eye, the nose, the whiskers, and the tail. Finish the legs and paws. Look at the model and redraw your sketch to make the lines smoother and more lifelike. And presto! You've drawn a cat!

Now you're free to color your drawing. You can also complete some big pictures, where you'll put several different animals in their natural environment.

While you are drawing, you will also learn many things about animals and their habitats. Look at the footprint left by the animal at the bottom of each page.

Cats on the Prowl

1 Draw an oval for the cat's body and another for the head.

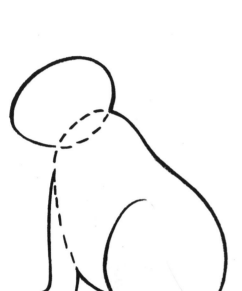

2 Look at the example and draw the legs and paws. Erase where you see dotted lines.

3 Add the ears, the eye, the nose, the whiskers, and the tail. Finish the paws. Compare your drawing to the example and redraw your outline to make it more lifelike.

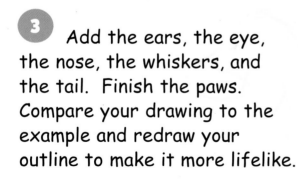

Humans have made pets out of cats. However, the family kitty belongs to the same group as the tiger or panther. As a predator, it has kept the silent, graceful walk and the hunting instincts of its wilder cousins, but it's still a playful animal.

9

Pick a Dog

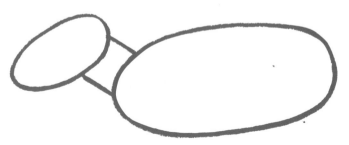

1 Draw a long oval for the body, a small oval for the head, and two lines for the neck.

2 Add a pointed tail and a bump on the head. Begin to sketch the legs. Erase the dotted lines.

3 Finish the legs and paws, then add the eye, the ear, and the dog's nose. Try to make your whole outline smoother. Now say hi to your new friend!

The dog that we love as a pet comes from, or is descended from, the wolf family, but humans tamed the dog long ago.

Since it can hear and smell well, the dog is a great hunting companion. Different breeds of dogs look and act differently.

Birds in Their Nest

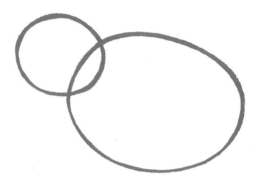

1 Draw a large oval for the body and a small one for the head.

2 Add the pointed beak and the long tail. Begin the legs. Erase the dotted lines.

3 Finish the feet. Draw a small, round eye and the wing. Look at the shape of your bird, then this example, and try to make your drawing clearer.

Birds build nests out of sticks and other materials. In many bird species, mothers and fathers take turns sitting on the eggs.

Once the babies hatch, both parents help feed them. They fly back and forth, bringing insects for those hungry, open mouths.

13

Spring in the Garden

After a long winter, spring has returned. Nature awakens, the temperatures rise, and the days get longer and longer. Birds migrate back to their summer homes.

Sap starts to rise in the trees and helps push the buds open. In early spring, the birds build their nests in the trees. A little later, baby birds hatch out of their eggs.

Chicken and Chicks

1 Draw an oval for the body and a circle for the head. The tail is a little triangle.

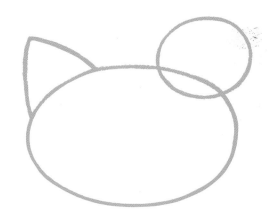

2 Add the beak and begin to draw the legs. Use your eraser to rub out the dotted lines.

3 Draw a beautiful comb on top of the head, the wattle under the beak, an eye, the feet, and the tail feathers. Can't you almost hear your chicken cluck?

Chickens scratch in the dirt for seeds and worms to eat. This barnyard bird has not known how to fly well for a very long time.

People all over the world raise chickens for their eggs and meat. Female chickens lay at least one egg every day.

The Duck Pond

1 Draw a large oval for the body and a circle for the head.

2 Add the beak, the wing, and a little, curved tail. The dots show which lines you can erase.

3 Make a round eye. Now look at the details on the example to finish your drawing. Look how pretty your duck is!

Ducks have webbed feet that help them swim. During the spring, ducks build nests near ponds and marshes. When the ducklings hatch, they are covered with soft feathers. The duck family leaves their nest and looks for food after the first day.

19

Bunnies on a Picnic

1 Draw two ovals — a large one for the body and a little one for the head.

2 Add two ears, the feet, and a puff for the tail, and the rabbit appears! Erase the dotted lines.

3 Finish your design by adding the eye, nose, whiskers, toes, and the inside of the ear.

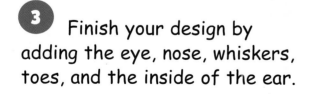

You might see rabbits in your backyard or nearby park, but rabbits also live in the woods. The female rabbit digs a shallow burrow, which she lines with dry grass and fur. Here, safe in her burrow, she gives birth to furless baby bunnies.

21

The Meadow in Summer

For many years, people have cleared forest lands, making meadows to graze their animals and fields to grow their crops. If they stopped working on the land, the meadows and fields would eventually return to their wild state. The bushes, for example, protect the farmland, but they also shelter all kinds of wild animals.

Silly Squirrel

1 Draw two ovals — a big one for the body and a smaller one for the head.

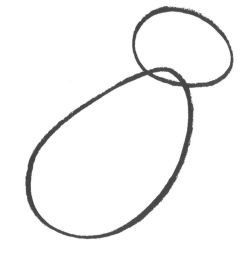

2 Add the beautiful tail and the back feet. Erase the dotted lines.

3 Complete your squirrel by drawing the eye, ears, nose, and front paws. Hey! Your new friend is ready to climb the trees!

The squirrel jumps from branch to branch and even goes down a tree headfirst. It eats nuts, leaves, and insects. If a squirrel has too many nuts to eat at once, it buries them. Sometimes the squirrel can't remember where it buried its food!

The Sheep Family

1 Draw a large oval for the body and a little oval for the head.

2 Draw another oval that overlaps the head. It looks like a hat! Add the ear and the nostrils, and begin the legs. Erase the dotted lines.

3 Add the eye and the hooves. Finish your drawing by making a beautiful, fluffy fleece.

The male sheep is called a ram, the female is a ewe, and the baby is a lamb. They graze on grass. Every spring, farmers shear the sheep and collect the wool. People make warm clothes for winter from yarn that is spun from this wool.

27

Cows in the Field

1 Draw a large oval for the body and a small one for the head.

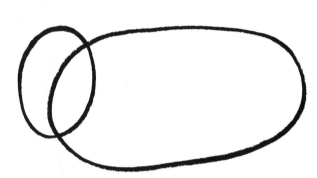

2 You are now going to add the horns, mouth, and nose and start the legs. Erase the dotted lines.

3 Next, carefully add all the details — the ears, eyes, nostrils, tail, udder, and hooves.

The cow is a mammal, so it feeds its calf with milk. The cow was first domesticated for its creamy milk. People also raised cows for their meat and their hides, from which leather is made. Cows eat grass and other plants growing in the field.

The Orchard in Fall

Apples drop from trees or are picked so we can eat them or bake them in pies. The squirrels gather nuts to store. The cows are still in the fields, but soon they will return to the warm barn. The birds have begun their long trip to the south. Fall has begun.

Donkeys

1 Draw two ovals — a big one for the body and a little one for the head.

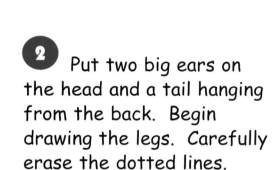

2 Put two big ears on the head and a tail hanging from the back. Begin drawing the legs. Carefully erase the dotted lines.

3 Now finish your drawing by adding the beautiful ears, tail, legs, and muzzle. Don't forget the little eye!

The donkey has long ears, a short mane, and a beautiful gray coat. It can climb rocky, steep paths more easily than a horse can. In many countries around the world, the donkey still carries people or heavy loads from place to place.

33

The Horned Owl

1 Draw a circle for the head, then an oval for the body.

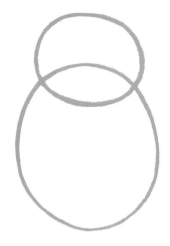

2 Add wings so the owl can fly. Then draw a tail and two funny ears. Erase the dotted lines.

3 Add the big eyes, a mask, and a little beak. Draw the tail feathers. The owl can grip a branch with its strong feet.

34

The great horned owl has powerful claws and a hooked beak. The two tufts on its head look like ears. They are made of little feathers that stand up. This owl is a raptor that hunts reptiles and small mammals at night and sleeps during the day.

35

The Forest in Winter

Snow softly blankets the Earth in winter. Wild animals adapt to the cold in different ways. Some animals hibernate, rolled in a ball in a nest in the Earth. Other animals find shelter in bushes and trees. If you take a walk in fresh snow, you can see animal tracks.

More to Read and View

Books about Drawing

I Can Draw That!: Easy Animals and Monsters (Books and Stuff). Robert Pierce (Grosset & Dunlap)

I Can Draw That, Too!: People, Places, and Things (Books and Stuff). Robert Pierce (Grosset & Dunlap)

Kids Can Draw Animals (Kids Can Draw). Philippe Legendre (Walter Foster)

Learn to Draw for Ages Six and Up. Nina Kidd (Lowell House)

Mark Kistler's Draw Squad. Mark Kistler (Fireside)

Mark Kistler's Imagination Station/Learn How to Draw in 3-D with Public Television's Favorite Drawing Teacher. Mark Kistler (Fireside)

Videos

Doodle: Drawing Animals (A & F Video)

Dan Mahuta: Drawing Made Easy (A & F Video)

Web Sites

Learn to Draw: tqjunior.thinkquest.org

Draw & Color with Uncle Fred: www.unclefred.com

Some web sites stay current longer than others. To find additional web sites, enter key words based on animals and habitats you've read about in this book, such as *cow, chicken, cat, owl, sheep, donkey, duck, squirrel, orchard, forest,* and *field.*

Glossary/Index

You can find these words on the pages listed.

adapt — to change to suit one's conditions or one's surroundings 37

burrow — a hole dug in the ground by an animal. An animal can live, hide, and give birth in its burrow 21

comb — a thick, fleshy crest on the top of the head of some birds 16

companion — a friend, someone who will go along with someone else 11

compass — a tool that helps draw circles. A compass has two arms — one placed at the center of the circle and another that holds a pencil 6

descended — from another kind of animal 11

domesticate — to train a wild animal so people can use or live with it 29

environment — the surrounding where an animal, plant, or person lives 7

fleece — the coat of wool covering a sheep 26

graze — to feed on growing grass and other plants 23, 27

habitat — the place where an animal or plant lives or grows 7

hatch — to come out of an egg 13, 19

hibernate — to spend winter in a state like sleep 37

instinct — a way of acting that an animal is born with and does not have to learn 9

mammal — a warm-blooded animal that gives birth to live young (not eggs) and that feeds them with milk from her body 29, 35

mane — the thick hair on the neck of some animals 33

migrate — to move from place to place. In the winter, many birds migrate to warmer lands; in the summer, they migrate back 15

muzzle — part of an animal's head, including its nose, mouth, and jaws 32

overlap — to rest on top of something and partly cover it up 26

panther — a large leopard with a black coat; a member of the cat family 9

predator — an animal that hunts other animals for food 9

raptor — a bird of prey; a bird that hunts other animals to eat 35

reptile — a cold-blooded animal with dry, scaly skin. Most reptiles reproduce by laying eggs 35

species — a group of animals or plants that have certain features in common 13

stencil — a sheet of plastic or cardboard with a design cut into it used to draw specific shapes or patterns 6

tuft — a bunch of feathers, hair, grass, or threads that are connected at one end and loose at the other 35

udder — a baglike organ on the stomach of cows, sheep, and goats that contains milk to feed their babies 28

wattle — a fleshy, wrinkled fold of skin hanging from the neck of some birds and lizards 16